CONTENTS

Chapter 1: Are You Really Ready?	1
Chapter 2: Do, Be, and Become	6
Chapter 3: Moments of Change	11
Chapter 4: Accountability	16
Chapter 5: Five Gold Goals	20
Chapter 6: Setting A Target and Target Practice	31
Chapter 7: Holistic Scaffolding™	37
Chapter 8: It All Starts With Awareness	42
Chapter 9: Developing Your Awareness Muscle	50
Chapter 10: Celebrating You	58
Chapter 11: Celebrate Being A Creator	64
Chapter 12: Accepting All of You	68
Chapter 13: Knowledge and Tools	75
Chapter 14: Triumphs and Tantrums	83
Chapter 15: Alignment	88
Chapter 16: Spirituality Sidestepping	92
Chapter 17: The Journey Continues	95

Legal Disclaimer & Terms Of Use

The information contained within this publication is strictly for research and educational purposes. The references included in this publication are copyrighted by their respective owners. If you wish to apply ideas contained in this publication, you are taking full responsibility for your actions.

Although you may borrow the "ideas" behind this resource, you DO NOT have resell rights or giveaway rights to any portion of this publication. This publication contains material protected under International and Federal Copyright Laws and Treaties. No part of this publication may be reproduced or transmitted in any form or by any means, electronic or mechanical, including photocopying, recording, or by any information storage and retrieval system, without written permission from the author. The information provided within this publication is for general informational purposes only. While we try to keep the information up-to-date and correct, there are no representations or warranties, expressed or implied, about the completeness, accuracy, reliability, suitability, or availability of the information, products, services, or related graphics contained in this publication for any purpose. Any use of this information is at your own risk.

The techniques outlined in this publication are the author's own thoughts and ideas, and should not be considered as a definitive set of instructions. There are no guarantees of success or specific outcomes.

Copyright © 2024 Laura Foster
All rights reserved. No part of this book may be reproduced or used in any manner without the prior written permission of the copyright owner, except for the use of brief quotations in a review. To request permissions, contact the author at:
laura@soulshealinghumanity.com
First edition November 2023

Please visit soulshealinghumanity.com for more!

CHAPTER 1: ARE YOU REALLY READY?

You may have picked up this book because the title grabbed your attention. Congratulations, you are starting to think like a warrior, a brave soul who has had enough and is ready to embark upon a fantastic sojourn.

With all the recent events and who-jazzy that humanity has been through, you may feel like you are a complete f*ck up, frustrated, and honestly, some days, you don't even want to get out of bed.

First of all, I want you to know straight up that you have never been f*cked up, messed up, or broken. And I know some of you out there are already defending your story. You're even ready to put this book down because you think I don't understand. I haven't been through what you have been through. Well, yes, you are correct. My story is different, but it definitely has a common thread.

There is absolutely nothing wrong with your True Self. It is your humanity that's been tinkered with, programmed, and conditioned. That is the part that is causing your discomfort.

By reading this book and "doing the work," you will see that you are just simply fed up with all the bullsh*t programming and conditioning your human has been subjected to your entire life.

Let's get things started on the right foot. I will define certain popular terms in a language you can understand. For example, in the previous paragraph, you read a very familiar and popular term: "Doing the Work"... If you're new to the journey, you may be like I was a few years ago, people would throw around these terms, and I'd be like, "Uh, that's interesting, Princess Woo-Woo, but what the f*ck does that mean?" Therefore, I'd like to highlight these terms and phrases throughout the book and define them in simple, easy to understand language.

Glossary: Wtf Does That Mean?

"Do the Work" We are all "doing the work," we go to work, do housework, and work out, but this is not what this really means. "Doing the Work" is a process of shedding your programming and coming into alignment with your True Self. (Don't worry, I'll define True Self soon.)

The universe gifted me an incredible framework called Holistic Scaffolding™ that you will use to create a life-altering plan for yourself. No, I'm not talking about something you read and then do nothing with. I'm talking about real, sustainable change. Yes, you are going to read things in this book that will shock you, that will piss you off, and will stretch your understanding and your limits, but isn't it time for that? Aren't you sick of staying in the same spot day after day, week after week, month after month, or even decade after decade?

How This Book Is Different:

In addition to the Glossary: WTF Does That Mean? The book is filled with;

Wisdom Nuggets:

This is sh*t I learned along the way that may be of some value to you on your journey. Yeah, these little nuggets may just come out of left field, hit you on the your head and leave you wondering, "What the f*ck was that?" Yep, they are meant to make you think, baby.

Wisdom Wands:

These are tried and true methods, many of which are variations of ancient practices, and will help you shed the human programming that has been holding you back from living your best life.

Holistic Scaffolding™:

The framework that takes the wisdom of our ancestors and great teachers and puts it together in a modern, easy-to-understand form that can truly transform your life.

Getting The Most Out Of This Book:

You will get the most out of this book when you choose to practice with what the Buddhists call "the beginner's mind." Many of the concepts and terms in the Holistic Scaffolding™ framework are familiar. However, it is how we utilize them that is entirely different.

Okay, you have had a lifetime of putting others first, saying, "Oh, yes, I do blah, blah, blah." when you really want to say, "F*ck, NO, I don't want to do blah, blah, blah!!" Isn't it time to put yourself first? Baby, I give it to you straight, no chaser. If you are already making excuses as to why you can't put yourself first:

> *I've got a needy partner.*
> *I work 120 hours a week.*
> *I've got a one-eyed cat.*
> *I am the ringleader of a three-ring circus, aka, my family.*

If you find thoughts like these rolling around your brain and continually making excuses why you can't show up for you, I highly suggest that you put this book down and either:

> *Give it away to someone who is ready to "do the work"*
> **OR**
> *Put it on your shelf for when you are really ready!*

Yes, I will share a revolutionary method to help you create your best life, but YOU must do the work. It is similar to hiring a fitness coach. They can design a plan for you, but, b*tches, you got to lift the weights!

Reading the chapters in order is essential, as they build upon one another. No, you will not use the Holistic Scaffolding™ in a linear fashion, but it will be presented that way for ease of understanding. And, once you understand this framework, the universe is the limit. Let's see what lofty dreams your True Self wants you to know!

CHAPTER 2: DO, BE, AND BECOME

Most likely, you live precisely as you have been programmed and conditioned for many years. And you may even be achieving many goals that were set for you or self- imposed.

For example, perhaps your parents always wanted you to become a lawyer. They saw that you were a little sassy f*cker, and repeatedly said, "You always argue. You should be a lawyer when you grow up."

Even when your dad would introduce you to someone new, he would say, "This is our Sarah; she's gonna be a lawyer." And guess what? That programming worked. What started as conditioning from your family turned into goal setting for yourself. And, after lots of time, energy, and money, you became a lawyer.

Now, I want to make this perfectly clear; there is nothing wrong with being a lawyer, especially if it is a profession that aligns with your True Self. More on alignment in a bit, but first,

Glossary: Wtf Does That Mean?

True Self:

This is your authentic self, your soul, your spirit, your intuition, your wise-ass motherf*cker that knows what's best. (Yep, and when you ignore the wisdom of your True Self and are out of alignment, sh*t goes sideways.)

However, you are not truly happy if you just became a lawyer due to your programming. Yes, you have the career; you may even have the partner, the McMansion, and the 2.5 kids (ugly truth, that .5 kid is a doozy). You are doing sh*t every day that is not in alignment with your True Self. And that is just one of the reasons for discomfort; okay, let's be honest here, your misery. I totally get you; I was there for many years.

Some of you are thinking, "Great, we've established that I'm miserable, Yippy-Skippy; I knew that before I started reading. So how do I start my journey?"

You need to begin understanding what your True Self really wants, and here's your first

Wisdom Wand: Heart Brain Coherence

More than thirty years ago, scientists discovered that there are neurons in your heart. If you're as old as I am, you grew up being taught that the brain was the control center. Well, it turns out that the heart is actually sending more messages to the brain, not vice versa. In addition, when you practice bringing your heart and brain into coherence in sync, you will actually come into tune with your True Self. And guess what? It's quick, easy, and FREE. (Confession time: I love free sh*t!)

How to create heart brain coherence:

Inhale into your belly for five seconds.
Exhale for another five seconds.
Repeat for three to five minutes.

I encourage you to do a deeper dive for yourself and learn more at
https://www.heartmath.org/

Okay, once you have practiced your first Wisdom Wand, tap into that wise-ass True Self and discover some things you want to Do, Be and Become as you move forward.

This is one of the first activities I completed to get myself moving in the right direction. But, truth be known, I still do this activity; yep, it's that powerful.

In this exercise, we're focusing on the journey ahead and the future us we can be.

> **Grab your index cards and a pen that brings you joy. (True Confession: I'm a gel pen addict.)**
>
> **Set your timer for 15 minutes.**
>
> **Answer the questions below, and put one answer per card**
>
> **Allow yourself to daydream.**

Make sure you commit to the full 15 minutes, you might be surprised what comes out!

What do you want to Do?
Do you want to visit Egypt, skydive, or find a new career? The possibilities are endless!

What do you want to Be or Become?
Do you want to be a better mom or a healthier version of you? It can even be as simple as wanting to be a baker or a reader!

Next, sort out your index cards into piles of 1 year, 3 years, and 5 years.

After you have completed the Do, Be, and Become activity, you will start to get a glimpse of what you want your life to be like moving forward. Take some time to journal about what you expected to come up and what surprised you. Keep those Do, Be, and Become cards handy, as you will need them when you begin to develop your own Life-Altering Plan (LAP).

Wisdom Nugget:

The universe will keep sending you the same type of lesson until you learn until you change, and until you come into alignment with your True Self. The places, events, and characters will change, but the underlying message will be the same. It's a recurring theme, and as you proceed in your journey in this book, you will become very skilled at noticing these repeating themes and patterns.

Let me share with you one of my moments of change.

Come with me for a moment to a frigid December morning in Michigan. I was in my early forties, morbidly obese, on several medications, and struggling. Even though I did not feel like it, I bundled up and headed out for my daily two-mile walk.

The night before, it had snowed, and the trees were glistening with heavy, wet snow. It was a complete winter wonderland, but I could not see the beauty. The truth was, I could not see the beauty within myself; I did not want to exist any longer. I must have been wandering for quite a while as my then-husband drove up beside me, rolled down the window, and asked, "Laura, are you okay?"

I distinctly remember saying, "No, I am not okay." He subsequently took me to the local ER, leading to a referral to a psychiatrist and several years of multiple medications to elevate my debilitating depression.

Spoiler Alert: Medications were not the answer for me. I had to bring my physical health to a state of well-being to start reversing my depression; more on that later.

Although this was an extremely painful and challenging time in my life, I can now see it was a beautiful moment of change. Even though I struggled, I intuitively knew I did not want to live with paralyzing depression moving forward; plus, I'm not a f*cking quitter, and neither are YOU!

If you can relate to my story in any way, allow me to guide you through the process. First, let's have you assess where you are in all sectors of your life. How are the physical, emotional, and spiritual areas of your life? Before moving forward, take your self- assessments at https://www.soulshealinghumanity.com/assessments.

CHAPTER 3: MOMENTS OF CHANGE

If you've looped around the sun enough times, you have most likely had some moments of profound change.

You have probably had moments that have stopped you cold. Perhaps, you were faced with the death of someone near and dear to you, and you could feel the shift in your reality. Unsure how you would take another step, another breath without them being in your physical space. Or, perhaps you've experienced a moment of clarity where you just can't f*cking take it any longer. You even contemplate just checking out and fantasizing about the quiet space beyond. No drama, no trauma, no pain, no suffering.

These moments of change are there for a reason. You do one of three things:

> *1. You can ignore them, sweep them under the rug and keep living.*

2. *You draw your line in the sand and use that moment to catalyze profound change as you move forward.*
3. *You snuff out your physical existence. (Not recommended; seriously, your presence is needed here!)*

How have you handled some of those moments of change in your life? Work Space

List three moments of change that you have experienced.
Moment of Change: Write what happened.
How did you handle that moment?

True well-being is much different than what we have been brainwashed to believe.

As humans, we have been programmed through advertising, society, social media, etc., to have a skewed view of what it means to have excellent physical, emotional, and spiritual health. I want to be very clear; there is nothing inherently wrong with any of the programming that billions of people live how they have been conditioned. However, you are different, you are noticing your own level of discomfort, and you are ready to peel back the veil of mass programming and conditioning. (You may be like me and totally surprised to see that the wizard behind the veil looks a sh*t-ton like that creepy little guy in the three-piece, green suit in The Wizard of Oz!)

Has Your Human Been Hijacked?

Let's get back on task and take a bonafide look at each area.

First, we regularly show physically fit people with ripped bodies with six-pack ABS, 10% body fat, and a tight round little bum. Again, there is nothing wrong with that as long as you are the one who is deciding that for yourself and not allowing some external programming to manipulate your human into wanting what someone else has.

However, let's examine what true physical well-being is. To truly be physically well is simply to have all the energy that you want every flipping day. You completely accept and honor this beautiful vessel you were given. You are rarely sick and have very few aches and pains.

Next, let's examine what we have been conditioned to think being emotionally well is. There is this narrative, a story if you will, that has someone always being happy, ridin' around on a rainbow and handing out lollies. Or, at the very least, someone who loves their family and laughing with friends. Think about any pharmaceutical or beer commercial. (A couple in matching bathtubs, riding off into the sunset. And, if the little purple ED pill really works, why are they in separate bathtubs? Shouldn't they be in the same tub, with a ginormous rubber ducky in the middle?)

I digress; true emotional well-being is choosing to be positive most of the time and consciously grateful for all you have. You also accept and honor all your emotions, the entire spectrum, from the suck-ass sh*t to beautiful bliss. And one of the most important things about your emotional well-being is you choose to learn from life. You actively choose not to get sucked into the vortex of goo that others can put out there for you.

Let's say one of your friends constantly energetically puts

out some nasty drama-filled goo; okay, let's be honest, it smells like a behemoth, steamin' pile of dog sh*t. Yet, even when you "step in" it, you choose to learn for it. Maybe your friend is teaching you how to set boundaries. You will read this a lot in this book: It is always your choice! You don't always get the opportunity to choose what happens in your life, but you do get to choose how to respond.

Lastly, we explore Spiritual well-being. Many of us have been raised in a particular religious faith following a particular dogma, tradition, and customs. Again, nothing wrong with that, as long as it is truly your choice and in alignment with your True Self. There is a massive difference between being spiritual and being religious.

Being Spiritually well involves living in alignment with your True Self, your Soul, and your Spirit. You live on purpose.

Glossary: Wtf Does That Mean?

Alignment:

The sh*t your human thinks, says, and acts matches what your True Self needs and wants. For example, let's return to your friend who's throwing down piles of dog sh*t. You think, "Oy, vey, I don't want to listen to so-and-so b*tch and complain again."
You say, "So-and-So, I've got to go and take care of some work."

Then, you end the conversation and choose to sidestep the

sh*t. Now, this is a simple example, and I know friendships can be very complex, but what is important is that you are coming into awareness of the choices you are making.

Once you have completed your Do, Be & Become cards and your assessment of your Physical, Emotional, and Spiritual status, are you ready to roll up your sleeves and start digging into the real tough stuff, accountability.

CHAPTER 4: ACCOUNTABILITY

Well, you're beginning to see where you want to go, and you have a clear picture of where you are physically, emotionally, and spiritually, and I bet you're tempted to jump right in and craft your life-altering plan. Uh, not so fast, Frances; first, we need to clear up some stuff that is getting in your way.

I'm certain some of you are Goal-Setting Gods or Goddesses, but you became a self-sabotaging puddle when it came to following through. We will explore the actual reason why this happens and, better yet, how to **never** fail at goal setting again.

From a very early age, we have all been conditioned to think that putting ourselves first is selfish and bad quality. Let me lay it right out for you. That's bullsh*t! Now, allow me to clarify that putting yourself first never means being cruel, judgmental, or insensitive to your fellow humans. Instead, it means that you align with your True Self and put those needs first.

You regularly show up for friends and family but often ignore your True Self and what is authentically best for you. For example, your family regularly celebrates a specific holiday. However, you have been exploring, noticing, and realizing that this particular custom is no longer in alignment with your True Self. Therefore, you decide not to attend this function.

Woah, we will discuss this more later, but be prepared. When you start living in alignment, some folks from your current community will flip their wooly wig. They will try to guilt and shame you into staying with the "tribe." They may even outright accuse you of being a selfish b*tch/bastard. They expect you to keep playing the role you always played. (Humans don't like change.)

It truly is your choice, and here are two possible scenarios:

You decide to listen to your Uncle Billy and not kill your Aunt Thelma by not showing up. She's got gout, a bad heart, and bad breath, and Uncle Billy insists that you not being in attendance will indeed lead to her demise. Therefore, you do what you have always done: attend the event. You are pissed off at yourself and don't want to be there. You drink too much wine and eat half a dozen cupcakes to numb yourself.

OR

You decide to listen to your True Self and politely announce you will not be attending the holiday celebration. You do not take the shame or guilt bait. You do not go into a long explanation about your choice not to attend. If you are comfortable doing so, you can offer to see the folks at another event without holiday customs.

Wisdom Wand: Just Say, "No!"

Here are three easy and simple steps to Just Say "No!"

1. **Be Present.**

2. **Speak from your Heart.**

3. **Be Brief** — There is no need to weave an elaborate explanation cloak.

For example, if you are asked to a party and don't want to attend, here's how you could respond.

Look the person in the eyes and say, "I appreciate the invitation, but I just can't make it." That's it; that is all you need to say!

Wisdom Nugget:

If you can't remember the steps or if you find yourself with verbal diarrhea, just: Stop, look down, and point to your left, yell, "Squirrel!" and run like your yoga pants are on fire!

As you consciously continue on this journey using Holistic Scaffolding™ and Wisdom Wands, all this gets easier. But for now, we have established that you regularly show up for others rather than consistently for yourself. Please do not feel guilty; you have been programmed that way, but there is a way out.

Let's get out some index cards, and on each card, write down one reason why you don't show up for yourself. Then, take some time and sort those reasons into the following categories:

Guilt Shame

Unworthiness Anger

Now, imagine putting all those reasons into a massive distillery. Let them simmer for about a week, a month, a year, a lifetime, and what do you think you will get? Oh, a nasty, vile brew that's, in reality, the underlying reason why you do not show up consistently for yourself.

Wisdom Nugget:

You don't unconditionally love and fully accept YOU! You do not value yourself enough to put yourself first!

Alright, I know some of you are sick of hearing about unconditional love; it's everywhere. You talk about it with your friends, your mate, it's on cute little social media memes, and you're like, "But how the f*ck do I unconditionally love myself?"

Patience, Pat, we are getting there. Coming into Awareness is the first platform of Holistic Scaffolding™, and there is an entire platform on Accepting All of You.

But before we delve into the Holistic Scaffolding™ framework, would you like to know a way to **never** fail at goal setting again?

CHAPTER 5: FIVE GOLD GOALS

Most of us are conditioned to set goals. We even have a particular time of the year that rolls around each January 1st when we dedicate ourselves to getting our sh*t straight and promise ourselves that this will be the year we finally lose weight, stop drinking, stop smoking, and stop giving the evil eye to the crazy barefoot lady in the cul-de-sac. Truth be known, I'm that lady.

Many of us still set New Year's Resolutions. If you are anything like me, I had lofty goals, but usually, by January 15th, I had given up on myself, sat back in the recliner, blamed others, and popped bonbons to numb myself. Here's the ugly truth about traditional goal setting: when we fail at any particular goal, we use that as a weapon against ourselves.

For example, let's say you set a New Year's Resolution to lose 50 pounds. You're all gung-ho the first few weeks, and then something happens. Maybe you break up with your mate and blame them for not showing up for you and doing the work. Some of your mental chatter may sound like this:

> "I was doing great until Sam acted stupid.
> Now I don't have a workout buddy and can't go to the gym alone.
> I can't diet with all this stress.
> I'm heartbroken."

Then, you use your perceived "failure" as a weapon against yourself. More mental masturbating:

> "I can never lose weight.
> All my family is obese; why do I think I can be any different?
> I hate going to the gym alone; I'm fat, and everyone stares at me.
> I'm such a loser."

Let's stop right there and put traditional goal-setting on notice! What if I told you there is a way to never fail at goal setting again?

There is, and it involves choosing to live by the Five Gold Goals. When you choose these goals, you will gain so much strength and power you will wonder where this knowledge has been all your life.

Wisdom Nugget:

These Five Gold Goals have been there all along; all the human conditioning and programming just buried them.

When you choose to live by the Five Gold Goals, you will always succeed because each goal is always obtainable. And they only rely on you. There is no external force that you allow to interfere. Each goal is a conscious choice.

Gold Goal #1   Choose to know the power of "I am."

Begin noticing what you are telling yourself:

I am brave.   *I am afraid.*
I am a badass.   *I am weak.*
I am a success.   *I am a f*ck-up.*

Uh, guess what? No matter what you are telling yourself, you are right. There is tremendous power in what you are regularly telling yourself. You always have the choice to use the power of "I am" as a statement of empowerment. There's lots of talk about getting your power back and stepping into your power; well, living by this goal is a quick, easy, and free way to do so.

Take a moment and fill in this statement: I am

Become aware of what you wrote. What are you telling yourself on a regular basis?

Gold Goal #2   Choose to align with your True Self.

True alignment is when what you think, say, and how you act is congruent. For example: you **think** about taking a hike,
you **talk** about taking a hike, AND
you actually **take** a hike.

Wisdom Nugget:

Being in nature is one method of being in alignment with your True Self, your spirit. Bonus points if you are barefoot.

You make this choice, and the moment you allow someone else to dictate something that is not in alignment with your True Self, you are giving your power away. Aren't you sick of that pattern? So let's look at a way to help you break it.

Wisdom Wand: Journaling

Journaling is a powerful Wisdom Wand, and it is so important to write things down. You are the author of your own story, and we will be exploring that in one of the platforms of Holistic Scaffolding™, but for now, get that journal out and spend time reflecting and writing about the following:

> *Become aware of times in which you are not in alignment. Perhaps, you are thinking and saying one thing, but then you are not following through.*
>
> *Reflect on each area of your life: physical, emotional, and spiritual.*
>
> *Are there areas where you are more frequently in*

alignment?

Are these areas where you are hardly in alignment?

Simply notice, without judgment, and write it down.

Gold Goal #3   Choose To Trust The Universe, Yourself, And Others

Choosing to trust the universe, yourself, and others is a potent goal. It can be a goal that can be difficult for your human self to grasp. Many of us have been brainwashed into thinking that sh*t happens to us, and we do not trust the universe. As you continue on this sojourn, hopefully, you will digest that the universe is always on your side Everything happens FOR you, not TO you. This is imperative for you to assimilate in order for you to exit the state of victimhood once and for all.

I know some folks are really stuck in their story; your brain is screaming, "But, you don't understand, this, that and the other, happened to me! I can never get over that."

Uh, you're right; if you are consistently telling yourself that and defend your story that stuff always happens TO you, very little will change in your life. Remember, the universe will keep sending you the same lesson, different people, places, and events, but the themes or lessons will be the same. That is until you actually choose to trust the universe and understand that everything happens for your most extraordinary unfoldment.

Wisdom Nugget:

When you first start releasing control and trusting the universe, it will feel weird, uncomfortable, and sometimes terrifying. Yep, that's me sheepishly raising my hand at the back of the local "Control Freaks Anonymous. Meeting." Like anything, you will get more skilled at trusting with practice.

Now, onto choosing to trust yourself, and this is an inside job. If you continue to look for external validation, learning to trust yourself will be as elusive as a rose-scented fart. But perhaps, you are thinking, "I always trust myself; I'm the only person I can trust!" Hmm, do you really trust yourself? If you continue to look for external validation, learning to trust yourself will be as elusive as a rose-scented fart.

Take the self-trust quiz on the next page. Check or highlight any of the concepts that ring true for you.

Top signs that you may not fully trust yourself

You do not understand and value your self-worth.

You constantly minimize your own needs.

You accept most of the negative, bullsh*t programming that came from your childhood.

You are constantly trying to prove yourself and your value to others.

You try to control everything around you so you can feel perfectly safe.

Sometimes it takes work to find, value, and/or use your own voice.

You are prone to find drama and trauma in every situation.

You repeatedly relive your past traumas.

You habitually have negative self-talk. (What a sh*tty soundtrack.)

You participate in behaviors that create additional shame and guilt for yourself.

You routinely break the promises and commitments you make to yourself.

You hold resentment and anger towards those whom you feel have "hurt you."

You constantly defer to others, asking what they think and what you should do.

This is coated with unconditional love, but if you checked one or more of the above items, you do not fully and consistently trust yourself. And that is holding you back.

When you truly Trust yourself, you can navigate anything, anyone, anywhere. Talk about being in your Power! You may be standing up, pumping your arms in the air, and saying, "F*ck, YEAH!" Then, you scratch your head and wonder, "But how do I do that?"

First Action Step:

You choose to understand the "Battleground." There really are two main battlegrounds to choose from

Freedom & Trust by "doing the work."

OR

Addicted to Drama ("Stuck in Your Story") If you want a deeper dive, explore how we become chemically addicted to our emotions. However, practicing Holistic Scaffolding™ will uncouple those addictions, and you will free yourself.

Understand that for every interaction you have during your waking hours, you can become aware of your chosen battleground.

Let's explore a specific example; someone cuts you off in traffic.

Freedom & Trust:
You may feel anger and frustration, but trust the universe that there is a lesson for you to learn. You choose to "do the work" and learn.

Addicted to Drama:
You feel the anger, react negatively, and repeat the drama, "Everyone cuts me off. Everyone's an idiot. I hate living here, blah, blah, blah…"

Wisdom Wand: Choosing Your Battleground

Reflect on something or someone who annoyed you in the past few days. Write what happened here:

Become aware of which battleground you are choosing. Circle One:

Freedom & Trust

Addicted to Drama

Write your thoughts, words, and actions regarding the annoying situation.
Now, reflect on any lesson you could have learned.

And, is there anything you would have done differently?

Second Action Step:

This is the step where you trust yourself and question everything! You will only grow once you venture out of your comfort zone and examine everything you have been told. Evolve or Repeat. It's always your choice.

When you do not trust yourself, you will NOT fully trust others. You will expect others to be as YOU want them to be, not as they are. You will expend a ton of energy on wishful, magical thinking! And, we ain't got time for that sh*t, now do we?

When you trust yourself, you have no issue trusting others.

Choosing to trust is essential; trust your True Self to navigate any situation and trust the universe is consistently working in your favor.

My dad bestowed an incredible piece of wisdom on me; he always said,

> *"Things always have a way of working out."*
> *- Bob Foster*

It is so true; you may not like how things will work out, but they always do. And this leads us to our fourth gold goal.

Gold Goal #4   Choose To Be A Life-Long Learner

Congratulations, by simply reading these words, you are already succeeding in being a lifelong learner. There are many profound benefits of being a lifelong learner.

It can improve your brain health; not to get too sciencey, but learning new stuff can stimulate new neural pathways, increasing neuroplasticity. Constantly learning can assist you in your career, relationships, well, everything!

One of the most powerful benefits of being a lifelong learner is that you can choose to come into alignment. And, when you do, you can share your wisdom with others to help them on their journey. Your knowledge can inspire and create a safe, nurturing space for your fellow humans. Isn't that what humanity needs right now, more love and compassion? So, let's go there.

Gold Goal #5   Choose Love

Choosing love can be obvious and is talked about widely, love, unconditional love for others and ourselves, but it can also be very ambiguous. Hang with me here; one of the platforms of Holistic Scaffolding™ will delve into genuinely accepting all of you so you can unconditionally love.

When you choose to adopt these Five Gold Goals, you set yourself up for success. No matter what, even if the universe sends financial, emotional, and physical challenges, you can always achieve these five goals and succeed. You do not have to rely on anyone else to be a champion of your own goals.

That can be a very liberating way to exist, but some of you may be thinking, "That's great, and I will try to live by the Five Gold Goals, but f*ckity do-dah, I want to get sh*t done too."

Oh, yeah! That's where we are going next. Setting targets to get stuff done on your journey.

CHAPTER 6: SETTING A TARGET AND TARGET PRACTICE

Crafting a life-altering plan (LAP) is choosing to live by the Five Gold Goals and becoming proficient at setting targets as you consciously and consistently utilize Holistic Scaffolding™.

Think of setting targets like playing darts. You would never expect to hit the bullseye 100% of the time, right? Well, that's precisely how you need to frame setting targets. We call it target practice, not target perfect.

You will begin to see that your target practice will become the chisel you use to chip away at all the programming and conditioning your human has received, just like Michelangelo created the fabulous sculpture of David.

Take a moment and reflect on what Michelangelo said,

> *"The sculpture is already complete within the*
> *marble block*
> *before I start my work.*
> *It is already there;*
> *I just have to chisel away the superfluous material."*

Just like Michaelangelo created the fabulous sculpture of David, you have the power to remove all the hard granite, aka programming, and present your stunning True Self to the world. And this is where Holistic Scaffolding™ comes into play.

Think about how many times Michaelangelo had to climb up and down the scaffolding, meticulously chipping away at the granite. If you choose to, you will be doing a similar thing with Holistic Scaffolding. It is a framework that has loads of ancient wisdom built in so you can set your own targets and uncover your True Self.

Now, your target practice is unique to you. No, I won't tell you that you should set this target and do these particular steps. I'm here to give you the framework. I want you to be aware of how you set your own targets.

For example, are you a traditional list maker who puts stuff on a calendar, or do you use modern technology to chirp, tweet, and buzz you to do sh*t? No matter what, the most important thing I want you to become aware of is:

Does your current method of setting targets (gettin' sh*t done) work for you?

If yes, keep doin' it, Douglas! If not, **STOP** doin' it, Denise! Whether you answered yes or no, there's always room for improvement. I'd like to share some things I have learned from working with hundreds of people.

How To Set A Target 101:

Set an Intention

Set a Time Frame

Celebrate YOU, Your Strengths

Identifying what Knowledge and Tools (Wisdom Wands) you need.

Holistic Scaffolding™

Reflect, Assess, and Regroup

Please permit me to walk you through this process, and then I'd like to share one of my student's target practice experiences that you may find helpful.

First, you need to have an intention. Simply put, you need to focus and aim for what you are doing or becoming. The caveat to not setting intentions is that we all live such busy lives that we can pull our focus and intention in a million different directions.

Modern humans are suffering from Intention Deficiency Disorder. But the great news is with Holistic Scaffolding, you can cease your own suffering.

Setting intentions is also a straightforward way to take your power back. I know this is a very popular thing in our society: taking back your power, stepping into your power, and empowering. I remember getting all excited as I'd read those phrases, memes, etc., and then be like, "F*ck. other than b*tch slappin' people whom I felt like were draining my power, I had NO idea how to do that." I digress, I don't think or feel that way any longer, and I am here to help you!

In addition to taking your power back, you will be shifting from the victimhood mentality to becoming the creator and author of your own life. You are the keyboard; you are the pen; what do you want your life to be? That's why you took time to complete those Do, Be & Become cards; sneaky, huh? I was already giving you a very powerful Wisdom Wand for setting intentions.

Therefore, what's one thing from your Do, Be & Become cards that you want to achieve? This is the thing that has the most energy around it. If you're having a hard time deciding, here's a suggestion:

1. *Take all the cards from the one-year pile.*
2. *Spread them out on the floor, okay, maybe on a table if you have pets or toddlers.*
3. *Now imagine you can only pick one card; what would it be? What has the most emotional charge around it? Pull that card out and write a positive, conscious intention right here, right now:*
4. *Next, setting some time parameters around your target practice is essential. It will help you stay on task and will help you avoid distractions and procrastination. However, one of the incredible things you will learn is why you allow self-sabotage and bail on your targets. But for now, just put a reasonable time frame around your target:*
5. *What time frame do you set for yourself?*
6. *Take some time to review all of your assessments; Emotional, Physical, and Spiritual.*

7. *What strengths do you already have to help you?*
8. *What knowledge and tools (Wisdom Wands) do you need to use or acquire? Reflect, Assess, and Regroup (Retry, if needed.)*

I firmly believe that we have a lot to learn from others. Sheila is a former student and graciously agreed to share part of her journey to assist you. Here's a glimpse of one of the first long-term targets that she set:

Target Practice:

What is one thing I want to achieve?

I will reverse my Type 2 diabetes.

What time frame do I set for myself?

One Year

What strengths do you already have to help you?

I love to cook.
I am determined.
I keep a positive outlook most of the time. I am a lifelong learner.

What knowledge and tools (Wisdom Wands) do you need to use or acquire?

I need to learn how to accept myself.
I need to learn how to stop blaming others. I want to learn breathwork.
I want to heal my inner child.
I need to find ways to manage my stress.
I will become a vegan.

I want to find ways to become more physically active.

Reflect, Assess, and Regroup (Retry, if needed)

I will take time each night to do a daily gratitude journal.

I will set appropriate targets as I use Holistic Scaffolding™.

To monitor my progress, I will complete the three assessments (Emotional, Physical, and Spiritual) once per quarter.

I will make appointments with my doctor to complete my blood work once per quarter.

Sheila wants you all to know that this was her first attempt at this type of target practice, and it is normal to feel frustrated with yourself. Practice really does make it better. "Practice makes Perfect" is just an example of bullsh*t programming you received, and from my perspective, it's just NOT true. This is just one of many pieces of programming you will be skilled at challenging as you proceed on your journey.

As you utilize the Holistic Scaffolding™ while choosing the Five Gold Goals:

1. I choose to know the power of "I am."

2. I choose to align with my True Self.

3. I choose to Trust the Universe, Myself, and Others.

4. I choose to be a "Lifelong Learner."

5. I choose Love.

And participating in target practice will alter your life in profound ways.

CHAPTER 7: HOLISTIC SCAFFOLDING™

> *"No problem can be solved from the same level of consciousness that created it."*
>
> *- Albert Einstein.*

Holistic Scaffolding™ is a technology that can bring you to a higher level of consciousness by utilizing different platforms. It will assist you in coming to the elevated vibration of gratitude and love. By celebrating your past triumphs and current strengths, you can shed away the exterior conditioning and reveal your True Self.

Simply put, Holistic Scaffolding™ is the framework, and the Wisdom Wands are your tools for chipping and chiseling.

It is essential to understand that while this framework is presented linearly, it is not practiced in that manner.

Keeping the creation of Michealango's David in your awareness is essential, as this is critical in successfully accessing the alignment platform for any area of your life.

Another profound analogy for using Holistic Scaffolding™ is the game of "Chutes and Ladders" or "Snakes and Ladders" for my British friends. (I'm glad I didn't grow up with the "Snakes and Ladders" version, as the concept of climbing up a ladder and then sliding down a snake would have creeped me out as a child and would have required a sh*t ton more therapy.) When you play "Chutes and Ladders," you continually climb up and slide down as you play the game. You will do the same in utilizing the Holistic Scaffolding™; you will climb up and down the scaffolding based on your needs.

HOLISTIC SCAFFOLDING™

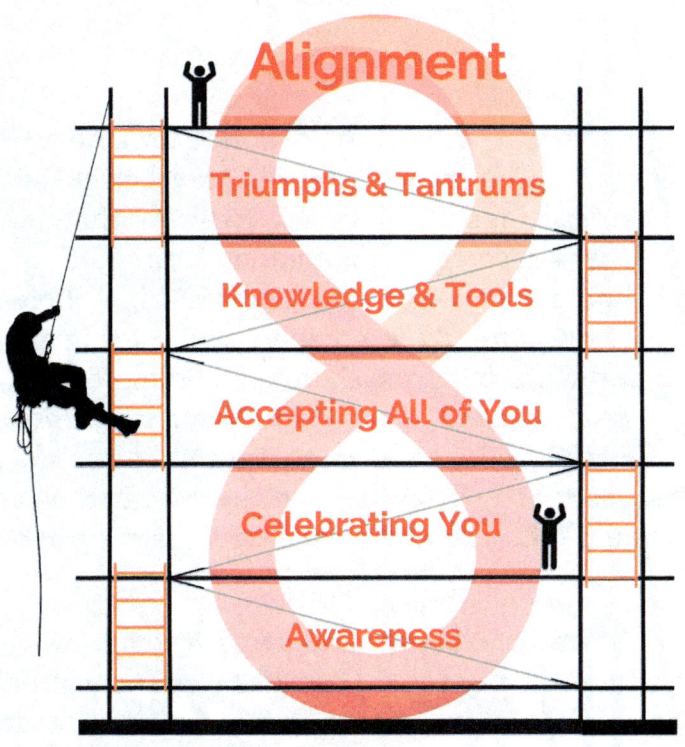

"The Sky's the Limit." You certainly have heard this phrase multiple times, but learning and putting Holistic Scaffolding™ into your daily practice will allow you so much more. I prefer to think of it this way, once you adopt the Holistic Scaffolding™ lifestyle, the universe is the limit. Okay, depending on your belief, you could ever say the muti-verse is the limit or your personal playground. You are way more powerful than you have ever been programmed to believe. You, yes YOU, can Do, Be & Become anything you can imagine!

I'd like to give you a little history concerning how Holistic Scaffolding™ came into existence. Travel back with me about 15 years ago to Florence, Italy. At that point in my life, I was severely depressed, and in addition, I had several different co-morbidity diseases: high cholesterol, high blood pressure, Type 2 diabetes, and sleep apnea. But to look at my life from a social media point of view, I had it all: a great husband, a wonderful daughter, a profitable career, and the ability to travel to Italy. But I was suffering; my life was mostly a facade. Social media can be a great mortician; it puts a beautiful face on something ill or even dead.

However, I was in Florence and decided to join my family on an organized city tour. The skies were gray, much like my mood, and as the day progressed, I just wanted to go back to the hotel room and sleep. However, we were scheduled to visit the Accademia Gallery, and something told me that there was something there I must see.

Therefore, I dragged my b*tchy, cranky, and depressed self through the gallery. When I first gazed upon Michaelango's David, I just stood frozen with tears streaming down my face. Other than seeing my daughter for the first time, this was the most beautiful thing I had ever seen. Yes, the gigantic sculpture embodies strength and beauty, but it was so much more for me. Unbeknownst to me, the incredible seed for Holistic Scaffolding™ was planted. Spending time in David's presence was a breathtaking reflection of what was lying within me, my True Self.

Through my journey, the Holistic Scaffolding™ was revealed, and it became clear that my mission is to bring this to help heal humanity. It is a gift for you! And Souls Healing Humanity is a society of people who are utilizing this method.

CHAPTER 8: IT ALL STARTS WITH AWARENESS

Before we dive right into the concept of awareness, I want to address one of the most common issues people have with making profound changes in their life: "I do not have enough time." As you proceed with the framework, you will notice that "time excuse" is just bullsh*t you tell yourself. Most of the platforms in Holistic Scaffolding™ do not take any additional time from your busy life.

In this chapter, you will learn several Wisdom Wands that can assist you in coming into awareness.

Whatever you want to Do, Be or Become, it all starts with awareness. This is the foundational platform. Your subconscious was programmed at a young age. All programming and conditioning are driving your life.

How did that happen? Well, it's been a constant stream of what you could and should do and believe. It has occurred in every arena of your human life: family values, societal norms, religious indoctrination, educational expectations, media, etc.

Most of it was not malicious, just humans passing along the programming they had received. (Not all programming is negative: Daily tooth brushing is a great habit, and nobody likes a stink-ass breath.)

Here's the trap: you may live unconsciously by someone else's rules and programs. And these programs may not be in alignment with your True Self. Remember, your True Self is your soul, your spirit, your intuition, your wise-ass mother f*cker. And when you are out of alignment, that is one of the reasons for your discomfort; okay, let's be honest about your misery and the possible reason why you numb yourself.

Awareness is the key to beginning to unravel the programming. And here's a Wisdom Wand to get you started.

Mind The Gap

True Self
What are some things that bring you bliss?

YOU

Programmed Human
What are some things that you have been told and conditioned into believing about yourself?

The closer the circles are, the closer you are to alignment.

Wisdom Wand: "Mind the Gap"

Begin to come into awareness in one area of your life. Look at the figure above and examine the alignment between your two circles. The further the gap between the two circles, the more discomfort you feel. Bring that into your awareness. Realize this doesn't take any more time from your day; you are just noticing.

A student of Holistic Scaffolding™, Brian, shares his experience with the Wisdom Wand: "Mind the Gap:"

> "I loved to dance as a little boy. I grew up in the 1970s, and when I would dance, my dad would tell me that only sissies danced. My friends played a lot of football and made fun of dancing, so I stopped dancing. It wasn't until I came to awareness that this was just the programming I had received and I had the spirit of a dancer. I now dance a lot."

Brian's brave story illustrates what many humans have been subjected to. Direct programming and conditioning to keep us in line, keep us in the tribe. But guess what? Most of the conditioning is not true. That is where your awareness is needed. If you genuinely want to come into alignment with your True Self, you must be willing to question everything. Yes, everything.

Does that match my True Self?

Does what I say express my True Self?

Do my actions reflect my True Self?

Is what I currently believe true?

Where did this belief come from?
(family, society, school, religion, etc.)

Everything is a choice! Once you become aware, it is your choice to continue to believe and live by conditioning OR change how you live. Some of you think, "I've lived with this programming for decades. How long will it take for me to truly come into alignment?"

Woo-Woo Alert:

The current energy is much more conducive to processing your drama, trauma, grief, etc., than it was just a few decades ago. The power of "I am" is always at work. You can choose and create the outcome: Which will you believe?

> **1.** *I am a powerful being that can access this incredible energy; I will come into alignment faster than I ever thought possible.*
>
> **OR**
>
> **2.** *I am powerless over what has happened to me. All this programming took decades, and if it is possible to reverse it, it will take a really long time.*

You are what you believe.
You are what you are telling yourself.
You are your actions.

Three Levels of Awareness

Awareness is consciousness, and there are three primary

levels. The first is the **awareness of self**. The self consists of the subconscious and the conscious mind. The concept of self can even be referred to as your ego. This egoic self constantly defines who you think you are. The perception of your identity makes you choose different roles and masks.

When you meet someone new, what do you say? It is like, "Hi, I'm Jerry; I'm a lawyer at Bent, Bitter, Begrudge, and Associates." It is the egoic self that is answering.

Wisdom Nugget:

I'm not a proponent of destroying your ego. From where I am in my journey, I still see value in being aware of your ego.

The next level of awareness is that of the **human collective**. As you move forward, becoming aware of what groups you belong to is crucial information. What groups do you identify with regularly?

> *Gender: I'm a woman.*
> *Ethnicity: I'm Hispanic.*
> *Religion: I'm a Christian.*
> *Nationality: I'm an American.*
> *Socio-Economic: I'm middle class.*
> *Education Level: I'm a college graduate.*
> *Politics: I'm a Republican.*
> *Sports: I'm a Detroit Lions fan.*
> *Hobbies: I am an avid reader.*

Uh, huh, you're starting to get the picture. Again there is nothing inherently wrong with being a member of any of those groups. However, just make sure YOU are the one being consciously aware of your participation. Is this the case, or are you simply choosing to remain in the group because that is what you've learned from someone else? This type of programming is very powerful because, most likely, your little human learned it at a very young age.

Did you know you were most impressionable in your first seven years on this planet? According to Dr. Bruce Lipton, during these early years, your brain operates at the theta and delta brain wave states. These are the brainwave states of deep meditation and hypnosis. Wowza, this explains a lot. Think about all the programming humans can receive during this time.

Let's say you grew up hearing, "Those damn old, white, rich, Republican men, they don't give a sh*t about the little people." Therefore, unless you come into awareness about the programming, challenge it, and decide to discard that from your belief system, how do you think you will feel when you meet an "old, white Republican man?"

Oh, people, we want tolerance, love, and peace. It's talked about almost continuously, but few know how we can get there. News Flash: Awareness is the key! Each of us must do our own f*cking work. You can not, nor have you ever been able to control anyone else. The Wisdom Wands presented will give you the tools to do your work!

The third level of awareness is that of the **multi-dimensional arena**. It is one consciousness: Love. From my current understanding, this is the level of the ascended masters: Buddha, Jesus, Krisha, Gandhi, Martin Luther King, and Mother Teresa, just to name a few. It is complex and something that I am continually studying and learning. However, it is so much more than just humans; this arena encompasses our true spirit, which is eternal and multi-dimensional. It also comprises concepts of sacred geometry and consciousbeings beyond my current level of understanding.

Why is Awareness the foundational platform for Holistic Scaffolding™? Simply put, if you do not work to establish a firm, secure foundation, no amount of self-improvement, self-love, or self-help programs you attempt will be lasting, and they will crumble. It is crucial to come into awareness as much as possible at each level: **Self**, Human **Collective**, and **Multi-Dimensional**. Will you spend equal time in each of the different levels? Of course, not. However building awareness is cumulative and ever-lasting. Here's a simple but profound example:

Have you ever noticed the arrow in the FedEx logo? Once you see it, you can NOT see it. This is just like awareness; once you learn a lesson, see something from a different perspective or decide to relinquish a particular belief, you are changed! It's always a choice. Are you ready for your next choice?

CHAPTER 9: DEVELOPING YOUR AWARENESS MUSCLE

Do you feel like someone or something is holding you back from living your best life?

Truth Bomb: You are the one holding you back. No one and nothing can hold you back unless you allow it to happen. Oh, I know this is a tough one to process, and it took me a long time to learn. When you choose to come into awareness, that is when you gain the gift of insight into what beliefs, values, and actions are getting in your way.

Let's explore another

Wisdom Wand: The Land of "Woulda, Coulda, and Shoulda."

Do you still live here? Are you still living in the land of

"I should have done this, I could have done that?" Living there is easy because that's where we were programmed to live. However, coming into awareness can help you pack your bags and move out. You deserve a respite, even if it starts with a short vacation from this oppressive land.

List all the things you think you should have, would have, and/or could have done. Then, examine that list and determine where that idea originated (my family, society, religion, etc.)

What would my True Self say?
What do I choose to challenge and change?
What do I choose to keep?

Now, here's an even deeper dive. In addition to judging yourself by the conditioning you received, you're also judging yourself by the current version of yourself. For example, I am 54 years old, and for many years, I harshly judged myself for staying in a relationship "too long." What I came to understand was that I was judging the younger version of myself with all the experience and wisdom I have now, at this moment. My younger self did the best she could with what she had.

Wisdom Wand: Watching Your Human

I saved the most powerful awareness Wisdom Wand for last, and it's called "Watching Your Human." I love this one because it doesn't take additional time to come into awareness. You watch what your human thinks, says, feels, and does.

Here's what I mean. Let's say your partner forgot to pick up your daughter at school, and you chose to call him on the phone and "bless him out." Your human is performing this action. Your True Self can sit back, come into awareness and watch it happen. You are not changing anything at the moment. You are just simply watching and becoming aware.

I know it sounds weird but stick with me. This ancient practice really works.

Now, don't go all "Judge Judy" on yourself. You are to merely watch your human without judgment. Notice how you think, speak, and act in any situation during the day. You become the silent witness, the observer. This method allows you to begin to access your True Self, the part of you that does not judge and accepts all that is happening.

One thing I do to remind myself to watch my human is I literally look at my hands. It helps me come into the present moment and observe what Laura is doing. Oh, she's a fun one to watch, and I often amuse myself doing so.

You may think of other tricks to bring yourself into awareness. For example, some people wear a rubber band and snap it on their wrists to bring them to the present moment. There is no right or wrong way to do this. The important thing is to practice a lot. Remember, awareness is cumulative; the more aware you are, the more aware you become.

Deeper Dive:
After you get the hang of "Watching Your Human," many other steps can enable you to take responsibility for your unhealthy programs and choose to change them. It's

always a choice: Evolve or Repeat. If you choose to evolve, you may find the following suggestions helpful:

1. Keep an objective, nonjudgmental journal of what you notice. You can even notice how others are responding to how your human acts. Do you see a pattern of justifying, defending, and rationalizing your thoughts, speech, and actions?
2. Track your emotions. Again, are you seeing any patterns? Frequent emotions in certain situations? Review the Shh Emotion Wheel on the next page.
3. Examine what is really true. Is this something you believe, or was it downloaded from your past?
4. Begin to accept responsibility for what is happening. Even if you perceive that the other person is 99% "at fault." Dig deep to find your 1%; it's there. You just don't see it yet.

Wisdom Nugget:

If you choose to place 100% of the blame on someone else or some other situation, it will stifle your growth. You can choose any one of these Wisdom Wands and develop your own targets around them. Perhaps, you set a target to "Watch Your Human" at least five times a day for five days and commit to recording what you notice in a journal entry.

In my observation, all humans are somewhere on The Awareness Continuum.

The Awareness Continuum

The Defenders:
These folks are essentially "asleep." They live the way

they have been programmed and do not question how they have been conditioned. They will readily defend that programming, and yes, that's where blind faith and/or blind patriotism exists. For example, the defenders grew up believing that a particular religion was wrong or this country is better than that one and will blindly defend their unquestioned beliefs.

The People Pleasers:
Humans, at this level, are aware of what others think and feel. They live by the conditioning but will only change if they feel threatened. If they think their tribe will reject them, they will quickly abandon any attempt to challenge their programming. These decisions are not guided by their True Self. As a result, they often feel "stuck," lost and overwhelmed.

The external locus of control drives the Defenders and People Pleasers. Simply put, they blame the exterior conditions for their own experiences.

Souls Healing Humanity Emotion Wheel

Wisdom Nugget:

If you take apart the word Blame... It's really to "Be Lame." The Defenders and People Pleasers assume they are powerless and some external force will control their life. Sh*t always happens TO them...They do not see or believe they are the creators of their reality, and very often react instead of respond.

Investigators:
The people at this place on the awareness continuum are watching their human. They are beginning to question everything, and do not blindly follow all of their programs. Beginning to peel back the veil, they are getting glimpses of their True Self. They question the situations they are placed in and can recognize the difference between external and internal locus of control. In most cases, they feel more empowered and choose how their human will respond, not react.

Awareness Warriors:
These humans strive to come into alignment with their True Self and constantly question everything. They view everything as a gift and choose to learn from every person, place, and situation. Even if the gift is a box of dog sh*t, they realize it is happening FOR them, not TO them. These warriors understand the internal locus of control and choose to live by the Five Gold Goals:

I choose to know the power of "I am."

I choose to align with my True Self.

I choose to Trust the Universe, Myself, and Others.

I choose to be a "Lifelong Learner."

I choose Love.

No matter where you currently find yourself on the

awareness continuum, remember you can move yourself to a different level. No one can do that work for you. Also, it is part of your journey to be at any level.

Wisdom Nugget:

When moving along the awareness continuum, It is not uncommon to become frustrated with others you perceive are still "asleep" or "behind you." This is a beautiful opportunity to practice compassion. Awareness is cumulative, but just like exercise, you must do it to build muscle and endurance. This is the foundational platform of Holistic Scaffolding™, and you will utilize it often as you progress on your journey.

Now that you have a basic understanding of awareness and some valuable Wisdom Wands to practice, it's time to climb, baby!

CHAPTER 10: CELEBRATING YOU

My deepest, most sincere wish is that one day you will love yourself enough to put yourself first. And, this is what the next platform of the Holistic Scaffolding™ is all about, Celebrating You! Unlike many other self-help programs that focus on the negative stuff you want to change, we are choosing to celebrate how awesome you are. In this chapter, you will learn three powerful Wisdom Wands that can help cultivate the celebration of YOU.

You'll learn how to bring yourself into the higher vibration of self-love. Uh, Oh, some of you out there just threw up a bit. I know you're sick of hearing about self-love. I get you. It can be as elusive as a rose-scented fart.

Glossary: Wtf Does That Mean? – Self-Love

Self-Love means putting your needs first and being responsible for your well-being (physical, emotional, and spiritual.) You fully accept all of you.

Wisdom Nugget:

Most humans are programmed to think that putting yourself first is being selfish. That, my dear, is pure bullsh*t! If you regularly put everyone else's needs ahead of your own, you are most likely not well in one or more areas of your life.

Isn't it time to draw your line in the sand and consciously put your needs first? This is authentic self-love.

Do you really Love Yourself?

Take a moment and scan this list. How many are true for you consistently?

I am assertive and say "No" when I need to.

I prioritize my physical well-being.

I prioritize my emotional well-being.

I prioritize my spiritual well-being.

My thoughts, words, and actions are in alignment.

I honor my voice and speak up when I am not comfortable.

I choose to nurture my fun and blissful nature.

I am positive most of the time.

I accept responsibility for my life.

I forgive myself for "mistakes."

I live by the Five Gold Goals:

I choose to know the power of "I am."

I choose to align with my True Self.

I choose to Trust the Universe, Myself, and Others.

I choose to be a "Lifelong Learner."

I choose Love.

I set reasonable targets and show up for practice.

I see every person and situation as a learning opportunity.

I love myself ENOUGH to keep moving forward.

Why is Self-Love so important?

Have you ever heard of the "Law of Attraction?" Yes, it's a "woo-woo" philosophy given from the universe to Ester Hicks. It states that you create your own reality. And that positive energy attracts positive sh*t, while negative energy attracts negative sh*t.

The law of Attraction is not scientific magnetism, where opposites attract. Though it may be true on a scientific level, it's NOT how the universe works for creating your best life.

It doesn't matter if you believe in this philosophy, but it is how things are operating in your life. For example, if you are trying to live a healthy lifestyle but constantly focus on the following negative things:

Body shaming (My butt's too big, I have thunder thighs, etc.)

Letting the number on the scale tell you your self-worth,

Telling yourself what foods you can't have

How sick and tired you are.

Telling yourself, "I can't eat healthy because I have to cook for my family."

Telling yourself, "I can't afford a gym membership."

These thoughts keep you in a negative state of mind and vibration. And guess what? You are attracting more of the SAME! So what are you attracting in each area of your life?

Wisdom Nugget:

Better or Bitter, it's always your choice.

Let's look at an example shared by Rosa:

> *"I was always running late and stressed out. I have three young children to get ready each morning. I yelled at them a lot. I was always putting them first, solving their problems. I didn't have a moment to myself I started putting myself first through Holistic Scaffolding™ and using the Wisdom Wands. I set a target to get up 30 minutes earlier, close my bedroom door and write in my gratitude journal. Not only do I feel better, but there is also much less yelling in the morning."*

Rosa came to understand that she was projecting her frustration onto her children. And, by choosing to put her needs first and to set a target of practicing the powerful **Wisdom Wand** of writing a daily gratitude journal - things shifted.

Wisdom Wand: Looking Back To Celebrate.

Instead of looking back at the things you "did wrong." Let's look back and focus on the things you "survived."

Remember, when tough times occur, they are not happening TO you but FOR your most extraordinary unfoldment. These times are NOT meant to paralyze you but to give you a fresh perspective. Sometimes to shake you awake.

What tough time did you "survive?"

What new skill or strength did you acquire?

Another way to bring you to a high-celebratory vibration is to do things you love. This may be obvious, but we often forget when we are so distracted by life in general. The next Wisdom Wand will help you have something handy to ensure you can quickly celebrate You!

Wisdom Wand: Bliss Box

Creating a bliss box is very simple. Grab some index cards and start writing things that you love to do. One important thing is that you take time to become aware of what your True Self wants. You may be wondering, "How do I do that?" Easy, think of something that you loved to do as a child. You did this to soothe yourself and to have fun, and you were in the "zone." Time seemed to dissolve, and you could do it for hours.

What you now view as childish, playful things you "shouldn't" do as an adult is just more bullsh*t programming. That thing you loved to do as a youngster is a significant clue to what your True Self needs and wants.

These are not the only Wisdom Wands to celebrate you. There are tons more. The essential concept is that to create the life you dream of, you must bring yourself into the high vibration of self-love. Otherwise, the universe will keep sending you precisely what you don't want, because that is what you match at a vibrational level.

You're well on your way to working your way up the Holistic Scaffolding™. There may be bumps along the way but you'll get there. There is no set time limit that you can spend on each platform and how you grow is completely up to you. I hope by now you've really started to see the value in yourself and when I say that I mean EVERY part of yourself. Until you see the importance in this we're going to stay right here and continue to celebrate you!

CHAPTER 11: CELEBRATE BEING A CREATOR

While on the Holistic Scaffolding™ platform of Celebrating You, let's explore what a fantastic creator you can become. It's imperative for you to understand that if you are not currently living a life you love, YOU have the power to change it.

By now, you realize I'm a no-bullsh*t kind of gal, and I will give it to you straight with no chaser.

YOU are whom you have been looking for! Krishna on a cracker!

Stop searching for someone to clean up your life.

Stop waiting for a magical politician to solve all the social woes.

Stop hoping and praying for world peace.

Stop being on tenterhooks awaiting a savior.

*Grab a f*cking broom and a mop, and your superhero cape!*

Start cleaning up your own "mess."

Start becoming a non-discriminatory and compassionate person.

Start cultivating your peace first.

Start realizing that you are your own savior!

YOU are whom you have been looking for!

No, this is not a typo. I really want you to read this again and again.

Step down the Holistic Scaffolding™ to the awareness platform and examine one self- defeating pattern in your life. What does it feel like when you bring that pattern into your awareness? Not so good, huh?

Now, I know saying daily affirmations is a big part of most self-love, self-improvement stuff out there, but here's the truth: You can say feel good, lollipops, and sunshine stuff to yourself all day long, but if you are feeling like sh*t and at a low vibration then not much is going to change.

Wisdom Nugget:

The Law of Attraction matches your vibration and sends you precisely more of what you feel, not think. That's why bringing yourself into a higher, more positive vibrational state is essential to creating a life you love. Moreover, until you understand that

You Are Whom You Have Been Looking For!

If you always look outside of yourself for the answers, it will lead to a rinse-and-repeat pattern. If you choose to think the same way, say the same sh*t, and act the same way, you choose to REPEAT, not EVOLVE.

You are choosing to evolve with Holistic Scaffolding™, and it is a life-altering plan. Before you can step into the badass creator that you really are, you need to shed some of that programming and conditioning. You must use various Wisdom Wands to assist you in clearing some of that negative energy that ultimately holds you back.

When you remove enough bullsh*t, celebrate you, and choose to live by this credo: Badass creators use positive thoughts that marinade in positive, potent emotions. You need to align what you think and feel to allow the law of attraction to help you create a life you love, not loathe.

Hopefully, you are practicing the Wisdom Wand of keeping a daily gratitude journal. It's so effective because you thank the universe for what you already have. Gratitude is a high vibrational state, just like love, and if you show gratitude, the universe will send you more of the good stuff!

Remember that the Law of Attraction always works. For example, if you're a Negative Nelly or Nick, the universe will send you more sh*t to shovel.

It is always your choice! You are always creating for yourself. So put yourself first and create what you really want and desire.
The only work you can do is on yourself. If you are still trying to fix others, you, my love, are "stuck" somewhere in the Blame-Game or Victim-Hood. Yes, you are creating

more of the same stinky sh*t.

Oh, Mother Mary on rye toast! One of the roles I played in my family was trying to "save" everyone. But here's the truth, all of that pouting, yelling, judging, and flat-out manipulation was just a major distraction that kept me from doing my own work!

Are there any family Saviors out there?
Please do yourself and them a favor, f*cking STOP trying to save them. Here's what you can do with your time and energy:

*Do your own f*cking work.*

Love them unconditionally.

Set your own boundaries.

Allow them to have their own experience.

Live by example (showing, not telling.)

See them well in all areas of their life.

Choose to Trust the Universe, Myself, and Others.

I am not saying these are easy choices; sometimes they feel heart-wrenching, soul- wrenching, but they are actually heart-revealing, soul-revealing. So what is this person or situation teaching you?

You may be starting to see parts of yourself that you don't unconditionally love and accept—time to level up in the Holistic Scaffolding™ and spend time on the Accepting All of You platform.

CHAPTER 12: ACCEPTING ALL OF YOU

Until you begin to accept all the parts of you, it will feel as if you are stuck. You know the feeling; you watch self-help stuff on YouTube, buy some courses, and do some work, but you are dealing with the same stuff six months, six weeks, or six days later. F*ckity-Do-Dah; isn't it time to put an end to that cycle?

You are Becoming Aware and Celebrating You. Now spend some time on the Accepting All of You platform for Holistic Scaffolding™.

Glossary: Wtf Does That Mean? – Acceptance

The official definition means to acknowledge any situation without judgment. At a deeper level, acceptance means you are conscious and recognize all parts of yourself. And, since we are all one conscious being, by honoring all aspects of you, you are also honoring all aspects of others.

Now here's where some folks just lose their sh*t! They are thinking;
"What? Why do you want me to accept all parts of me, even those parts I don't like? If I accept everything, then I won't change."

Christ on a cracker, calm down. I never said things wouldn't change. It's the human programming and conditioning you are working to be aware of and challenge. That most definitely will change. You are becoming a master creator of your own life.

Look at the Figure and review the difference between your TRUE Self and you that lives by your human programming and conditioning. You can think of your True Self as "The Sky;" it is the backdrop for all the weather. "The Weather" is all the bullsh*t programming and conditioning—the Land of Coulda, Woulda, & Shoulda.

You are not the weather! YOU are the sky!

The sky does not judge. Can you imagine how absurd it

would be for the sky to get mad at the storm?

Sky:

> *"Clouds, you're pissing me off today. I told you never to appear on a Tuesday.*
> *We even had therapy about this, and you agreed you would only show up every third Wednesday. And, boom, there you are being passive-aggressive again and showing your white, fluffy puff-ball ass.*
> *What the f*ck is wrong with you?"*

Nope, that is not what the sky does. It just sits back and accepts all that is. Ultimately, it knows all will change. No storm is permanent.

Henry Wadsworth Longfellow says it best;

> *"For, after all, the best thing one can do when it's raining is let it rain."*

When you understand that your True Self is the Sky, you can come to a place to accept all of you entirely. Knowing your True Self, you will understand that:

You were never broken.
You are NOT broken now.
*You are not f*cked up.*
*You are fed up with all the bullsh*t your human has endured!*

By now, you are regularly on the awareness platform, watching your human. You may even notice some patterns. Believe it or not, we all have multiple personalities. I call them players or characters. To reach any level of alignment, enlightenment, and peace, you must come to accept and understand ALL of your players, all of you. Although we play many different roles and put on tons of masks, there are three main archetypes of Players:

The Closet Character:

These are parts of you that you exiled to the closet. You hid them away for whatever reason. Trauma, pain, or fear could lead to this part being isolated or hidden to be kept safe or simply to remain part of the tribe; this would undoubtedly be vitally important if you were an infant, unable to care for yourself.

The Multi-Tasking Master:

This is the *B*tch as Mutter F*cker that gets sh*t done! They are in charge of the day-to- day operation of your life. They can also set targets, help you focus, and achieve a sh*t- ton of stuff. There is also an "ugly" side that can show up as a control freak or Judgmental Judy.

Dictating Distractor:

Or, as I affectionately call her, "Squirrel."
When an exiled closet character gets triggered, the dictating distractor will swing into action and suggest all sorts of sh*t to remove the focus from potential "pain," food, business, alcohol, drugs, technology, etc.

All these archetypes are part of your human. They serve a purpose, but sometimes, their services are no longer needed. It is now your job to unconditionally love and accept all the parts of you. No one else can do this for YOU!

Okay, great information, but where do I start?

Back to the Awareness platform.
Take time to notice and reflect:
What roles/ masks do you wear daily?
What archetype are they?
What is their true purpose?
Are they needed any longer?

Here's a very personal glimpse of my journey. I have a predominant Closet Character archetype whom I call Little Laura. As a young girl, I was sexually abused, and Little Laura had many different roles, but the one that kept recurring was protecting me. She kept constructing a massive heart wall that reminded me that "Men Can't be Trusted."

While Little Laura was just doing her job, "protecting me," I realized how she was limiting my ability to connect with people on a heart level. This took some work, but in a nutshell, I thanked Little Laura and let her know she no longer needed to protect me. I had to remind her that I'm a grown, wise-ass woman. And all she has to do now is play and have fun. I love her. I do not doubt that working with this process will produce powerful results, and I encourage you to share your story. You are not alone!

Now that you are aware of some of your characters, let's explore another Wisdom Wand.

Wisdom Wand: "You Annoy Me; I Love You!"

Some of your biggest annoyances are your most significant gifts. First, they can bring awareness of your character at work. Then you can choose to "heal and help" them and begin to set yourself free.

When someone or some situation annoys you or pisses you off, come into awareness and contemplate which reason is valid:

*Is it a reflection of sh*t you have not dealt with yet?*

OR

*Is it sh*t you have dealt with, and is it a reminder to celebrate you and practice compassion for the other person?*

You see, you still love them no matter what reason you choose. They are helping you, and you are choosing not to play the blame game.

Furthermore, we are never blaming or shaming the characters in our lives. We have had a lifetime of doing that, which didn't work well for me. These players were doing the best they could in any situation.

Accepting All of You is a different approach. It allows space for all players to understand and appreciate their role in our lives. It's your choice. Can you release them from the role they have played, or is their role still necessary?

Imagine becoming Aware, Celebrating You, and Accepting all of your parts. Now, this is a place of megawatt power. Next, we are climbing to the Knowledge and Tools platform for more transformation.

CHAPTER 13: KNOWLEDGE AND TOOLS

One of the Five Gold Goals is to choose to be a lifelong learner, which is the Holistic Scaffolding™ level that nurtures that concept. Gaining more knowledge is critical to your journey towards your best possible life.

Wisdom Nugget:

If you haven't had a major change in your thinking in the past year, check your pulse, you may be dead.

There are tons of people who choose to live exactly as they have been conditioned.

They live in the same region of the country, the same state, or even the same neighborhood as their parents.

They cheer for the same sports team as their friends and family.

They hate the same type of people.

They go to the same place on vacation.

They attend the same church, or at the very least, they participate in the same religion.

They keep the same traditions and customs.

They follow the rules even when the rules don't make sense.

Uh, you get the picture.

Again, I want to emphasize that there is nothing wrong with living as you have been programmed. Even the folks out there that hate other people, while I disagree with that, it is not my job to judge their choice. Remember, the only work you can do is on yourself and live by example.

However, you are different! You are realizing that you are fed up with the way your life is unfolding. Congratulations! You are here, you are learning, and this takes tons of courage.

As you begin to question and shed some of your programming, I want you to be aware that things will get uncomfortable. Perhaps, some of you have already felt the discomfort and have been "rejected" by your friends and family, and it hurts! Maybe you have always been the "Black Sheep" of your family, or perhaps it is a new label (I like to call it a True Badge of Courage.)

Along with this label usually comes a few other designations: batsh*t crazy, nuttier than Aunt Thelma's fruit cake, lunatic, unhinged, etc. Do any of those sound familiar?

You sometimes feel like no one on the planet gets you, and you just want to curl up in your closet and cry. Yes, "Closet Crying" is a real thing.

Know that the pain and discomfort you are feeling is just your human grasping onto the pain of "rejection" and "abandonment" to try and get you to keep following your programming and remain part of your tribe. Your human is just trying to fit in, and a level of fear keeps you from shedding those layers and aligning with your True Self.

I lived for years, okay decades, being afraid of showing people who I really am, being my True Self, allowing my uniqueness to shine, and being unapologetically a disruptor. So I totally understand the suffering and agony you may be feeling.

Wisdom Nugget:

The conditioning and programming are fierce and relentless. When you start to veer from your tribe, you will be "rejected." For example, if it's been a family tradition to attend an annual religious service, but through your own study, this is no longer in alignment with your True Self, and you decide not to attend this year. Oh, Krishna, on a cracker, you will get an earful, and some family members will try to shame and/or guilt trip you to get you "back in line."

Be brave; you now have Holistic Scaffolding™, Wisdom Wands, and the Souls Healing Humanity Society to utilize as you continue your lifelong journey.
It's always YOUR choice; you can continue to follow all

of the conditioning and programming set in place by your family, friends, and community, or you can question everything. You can decide to set out on your own Hero's Journey and shed all the bullsh*t programming that is holding you back. No one forces you to take this path; however, if you do, be ready for some drama from others. Yes, there will be ups and downs on your journey, but once you've shed enough of your bullsh*t programming, you will no longer care about the labels and judgment of others.

Now let me be clear, you are always kind, compassionate, and respectful to the ones who judge you, but you remain steadfast to your mission, and you do not waiver from your ultimate goal of freedom and "enlightenment."

Wisdom Nugget:

All the labels and lectures you will receive are just a reflection of things the other humans need to process. For example, loads of people judge my barefooted-ness. I intuitively know they are just living as they have been programmed and truly don't know it's okay not to wear shoes. No judgment here for them, only love.

As you continue your journey, you will come to a place where you embrace your uniqueness and realize it is a gift. Firstly, to yourself, because you no longer have to wear those masks and play roles you disdain. You are FREE to get up in the morning and just be unapologetically YOU!

Secondly, your uniqueness, being a disruptor, is a beautiful contrast to other humans. When you show up as your True Self, this may illustrate a profound dissonance that is festering within them. You may just be the trigger they need to heal some of their drama and trauma.

In addition to continual learning, you will need tools, or Wisdom Wands, to chip away at all that programming so that you can see your True Self. If you can't get glimpses of your True Self, how can you ever expect to come into alignment? Let's explore some additional Wisdom Wands:

Wisdom Wand: Meditation (Yoga Nidra)

I'm sure you know there are tremendous benefits to meditation. No, I won't ask you to sit on a meditation cushion, chant "Om," and empty your mind. (Nothing wrong with that.)

Your experience may be similar to mine. Many years ago, I tried to meditate. I purchased an expensive cushion, an eye pillow, and a meditation CD. I really tried, I honestly did, I got out of bed early, got myself all settled, and the monkey chatter was consistent. I was never able to empty my mind. My experience with meditation left me frustrated, and eating a half gallon of Moose Tracks ice cream; I haven't always been a vegan.

However, I have found the most accessible and beneficial form of meditation to be Yoga Nidra.

Alright, I can hear some of you saying, "F*ck, did she just say the word yoga? Uh, I don't do yoga. My legs don't fold that way any longer, uh, well, they never folded that way. I once tried a yoga class, and I couldn't flippin' walk upright for a week. So, nope, not doing it; no, thank you."

I'm gently taking your hand and lovingly walking you away

from the ledge. It's okay; we are not talking about that type of yoga. You are literally going to lie down on a mat, recliner, or your comfy bed and do NOTHING! Then you listen as a practitioner guides you to complete relaxation.

The term yoga nidra translates to yogic sleep. You will not be sleeping but will be guided to the theta brainwave state. This is where you can shed conditioning and reprogram your subconscious. I encourage you to learn more about yoga nidra. It is my spiritual practice that I practice the most frequently.

Wisdom Wand: Emotional Freedom Technique (Eft And Tapping)

This is another of my personal favorites that I practice daily, sometimes several times per day.

The Emotional Freedom Technique is based on ancient Chinese acupressure and modern psychology to manage stress, improve sleep, relieve pain, and more. It literally takes a few minutes to learn.
It is free (I love free sh*t, don't you?) It is easy to learn.
It has tons of scientific studies to back up the claims.
It really works. However, it's just like anything. If you don't do it, it will NOT work!
I highly encourage you to explore this power tool.

https://www.thetappingsolution.com/

Wisdom Wand: "The Poop Process"

Oh, this one has a fun name and is very powerful. Let's

dive right in; no pun intended. When someone pisses you off, give this a try.
Drop back to the Awareness platform and notice what you are feeling.

Name the emotion.

Give that emotion an intensity number from 1 to 10.
1 = "Hardly Feeling It"

10 = "It's Totally Taken Over Me!"

* Did you know that the average emotion only lasts 90 seconds?

Feel it; literally, sit with it. Avoid the trap of the Dictating Distractor. (You know, checking your phone, answering the call of your recliner, and checking out with games, Netflix, etc.)

Explore the Perspectives of "The Story" attached to the emotion… from three different chairs:

- **You**
- **Them**
- **"Joe Friday"**

First, visualize sitting in the "**You**" chair; now, tell yourself the story from your own perspective. Don't worry about judgment here; let it all out.

Next, sit in the "**Them**" chair and tell the story from their perspective.

Lastly, sit in the "**Joe Friday**" chair and tell the story with "Just the facts, ma'am'"

Use Dynamic Holistic Scaffolding™ to digest this emotion and release the attached story. What additional Wisdom Wand can help?

Heart Brain Coherence.

"You Annoy Me; I Love You!"

Emotional Freedom Technique (Tapping.)

Then, "Poop it Out" and Let that sh*t Go!

Wisdom Nugget:

One of the caveats of human behavior is that we are addicted to our drama. (Look this up: scientific evidence proves this is true.) Even after we have "dealt" with sh*t, we look at it, smell it, poke it, and instead of walking away, we pick it up repeatedly. Trust the process; you can overcome your sh*t.

These are just a sampling of some of the tried and true Wisdom Wands I have used over the years. Keep trying and exploring the ones that work best for you. Stop looking for approval from others. If your "woo-woo" sh*t bothers them, that is their problem. Love them anyway, and keep doing your own work!

By now, you are accumulating so much knowledge and loads of Wisdom Wands to assist you as you chisel away from the bullsh*t programming to reveal your True Self. Let's clammer to the next Holistic Scaffolding™ level: Triumphs and Tantrums.

CHAPTER 14: TRIUMPHS AND TANTRUMS

Have you noticed that there is a vertical infinity symbol in the background of the Holistic Scaffolding™? That is not by accident. Holistic Scaffolding™ is a lifestyle choice, and you will constantly climb up and down the framework. Although the levels have been presented in a linear fashion, you will not be using them in that manner.

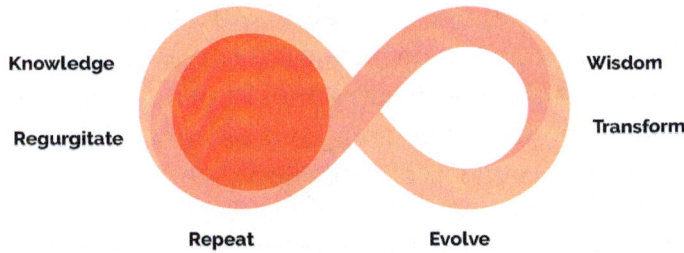

How you live your life is always a choice. Previously we discussed how you choose to be Better or Bitter, Evolve or Repeat. Most humans remain in a repeat cycle. Hells Bells, I lived in the repeat cycle for decades.

The repeat cycle looks like a vicious circle because it is. You may learn tons of information and be able to regurgitate what you learned with great accuracy, but very little actually changes in your life. You even have those "Oh, f*ck me sideways" moments and times when your life literately falls apart in front of you. The universe is sending these events to wake you from your slumber. However, many of us realize something isn't right and even attempt to change, but we stay on the repeat circular side. It takes something like implementing Holistic Scaffolding™ and Wisdom Wands to bring you to the place where you can Evolve! This is where you start to come into alignment with your True Self and tap into true wisdom. This infinite loop allows for the authentic transformation you have desired for so long.

When you choose to continually evolve, your sojourn will have many valleys and peaks. This is where you can just pause on the Triumphs and Tantrums platform. Just like we are learning to accept all of our human characters and all of our emotions (even the ugly cry), we also need to learn to accept the full spectrum of experiences, from the winning moments to the ones that bring us to our knees. They are all so crucial to our mission.

One question often arises: How is Celebrating You different from the Triumph platform? On the Celebrating You level, you honor what your human has accomplished; you also learn to celebrate the small wins and your positive character traits.

Example: I set a target to write in my gratitude journal daily for one month. I achieved that target, and I am celebrating ME! Being on the Triumph platform is different. Yes, you are celebrating, but this is reserved for when you have been working hard to overcome a bit of programming or a self- defeating pattern or habit.

Example: I have been using Holistic Scaffolding™ and Tapping to address my substantial self-limiting belief: "I'm not smart enough!" I have finally shed that belief. I pinpointed where it came from and learned how to clear all the negative emotions attached to that false belief. I know now without a doubt that "I am one smart cookie!" (I love cookies!)

Triumphs are great, but there is also another area of this platform: Tantrums. Oh, let me warn you, they are going to happen. You are going to say things like:

*F*ck this sh*t!*

I'm done!

I quit!

*I'm too f*cked up.*

No one understands what I went through.

I'm not interested in learning anything else.

*You can take all your third-eye, woo-woo, enlightenment sh*t and shove it up your ass. I'm OUT!*

Okay, I'm confessing that I had several tantrums along

the way. I even took all my self- help books and journal and threw them in the trash. It was a tough couple of weeks, but I allowed this tantrum to play out. There were even times when I was suicidal; I felt like my time on this planet was a tremendous waste of time. I chose not to seek "professional" help as my previous experience with antidepressants was not a route I was willing to take.

I came to understand that part of my human was ready to "die off". It was part of my metamorphosis. I was shedding part of the old me so my next upgraded version could arrive. And it did! I learned so much from this experience; I truly see it as a gift. However, if you do find yourself at the Tantrum platform, here's a Wisdom Wand that may help.

Wisdom Wand: Hit The Pause Button

You need time to rest, reflect and rejuvenate. Allow for the full spectrum of the emotions you are feeling. Find ways to nurture yourself consciously:

Take a warm bath.

Spend time in nature (barefoot.)

Go to bed early or sleep in.

Give yourself an extra long hug.

Wisdom Nugget:

The longer you stay dedicated to Holistic Scaffolding™ and diligently working your Wisdom Wands, the less frequent and intense the Tantrums will be.

But by choosing the infinite loop of Holistic Scaffolding™ and the Wisdom Wands, you will transform your life. You will evolve and come into alignment, which is where we are headed next.

CHAPTER 15: ALIGNMENT

You will reach the platform of Alignment numerous times on your journey. Alignment is where you know your True Self and your thoughts, words, and actions are the same. You have shed enough of your programming to allow your True Self, soul, and spirit to shine through. This is what I refer to as Authentic Enlightenment. Your True Self is unconditional love; it is pure light, pure energy, and allowing that to shine through to others is our real purpose.

Nope, you didn't come here to accumulate stuff, wear fake masks, and unquestioningly follow the rules and religious dogma.
You came here to learn!

Nope, you did not come here to judge yourself or others.
You came here to LOVE Unconditionally!

Nope, you didn't come here to repeat programming and convert others to your way of thinking.
You came here to Shine for yourself and others! (What they do when they are in the presence of your light is

their business.)

It is essential that when you reach the platform of Alignment, you remain humble. Nothing is worse than being very overweight and having a friend lecture you about their new diet and how much weight they have lost. Yeah, I know you want to b*tch slap them, but you now have the Wisdom Wand "You Annoy me; I Love You!" to keep your ass out of jail.

Holistic Scaffolding™ is a lifestyle choice, and we all now clearly understand: The only work we can do is on ourselves. We can't do someone else's work! We create our own reality. We can NOT create someone else's reality! There is never any need to preach to someone else. You are not responsible for their journey. You are never expected to convince somebody that they should follow the principles of Holistic Scaffolding™. Yes, if they are curious about your transformation and ask questions, of course, share your knowledge, but it is never in an evangelical manner.

I am not a guru; you are your own guru! And I sincerely hope that you have learned that you can never be someone else's guru or savior. They have to do that for themselves. You can only become authentically enlightened and live by example for them. Again, what they do with your brightness is *their* business; release yourself from the pressure you need to save them. You can NOT!

Alignment and Authentic Enlightenment can happen in any area of your life: Let's examine what it could look like in each of the areas:

Physical:

When you reach alignment in the physical realm, you

achieve one of your targets. For example, perhaps you set a target to reverse your Type 2 Diabetes. You no longer think or speak to yourself or others like a person with diabetes. Your actions match being a non-diabetic (great food choices: I recommend being a vegan. And moving a lot!)

Emotional:

Once you achieve an emotional target, you will be at the Alignment level. Emotionally, you become well, and people notice how calm and balanced you are. (Even in the chaos that is happening all around you.)

Spiritual:

When you become spiritually well, family, friends, and strangers will notice how at peace you are. You vibrate a level of compassion and unconditional love. You are living ON purpose. You are daily living your true mission for this lifetime.

It is crucial that you remain humble and not boastful or preachy about your achievements. Trust the universe that whoever is supposed to know about your victories will learn about your challenges, restored health, or life's purpose.

I truly believe that when we reach the Alignment: Authentic enlightenment level, we discover life's purpose and live each day **On Purpose**. This is why we came to this time and place to shed all the bullsh*t and realize we are pure love, pure energy, and incredibly powerful beings. **You are whom you've been looking for!**

Reaching the Alignment: Authentic Enlightenment

platform, you are able to answer the age-old question: "Who am I?"

Spoiler Alert: You are a unique spiritual being having a human experience. You rightfully and unapologetically step into your full power from this place!
Many humans still believe that they are humans who have occasional spiritual experiences. Nothing wrong with that belief, but it is so limiting. Believing that you are simply a meat-covered skeleton that sometimes has a spiritual practice still places expectations, wishes, and prayers on an external force, you see?

When you begin to align with your True Self, you know at the quantum level that you are the creator of your reality. You are a powerful being!

You are whom you've been looking for!

Not all in this lifetime choose this path or can see their true potential. They still choose to live by the old paradigm, and that is perfectly fine. Not all humans are able to free themselves; many still feel they need a doctrine or dogma to follow. This can lead to a warning zone that I call "Spirituality Sidestepping."

CHAPTER 16: SPIRITUALITY SIDESTEPPING

Many, many wars have been caused by religious intolerance. For humans, there has been a long history of being grounded in a particular faith and criticizing others who do not believe as they do. And it's not only religious beliefs that have pitted humans against humans. It's all the programming of not honoring the differences between us. We constantly separate ourselves by our differences. We have had several millenniums of this way of thinking, which has taken a massive toll on humans. Many of us intuitively know it is time for a change.

The universe gifted Holistic Scaffolding™ to help heal humanity. It is a technology to help you discover your True Self. And, all the wisdom that you have learned here has never been a rigid doctrine to follow; I hope that you choose to live the Holistic Scaffolding lifestyle to birth a new existence for yourself. One where you authentically know your True Self and align with that spirit.

This is where tolerance exists.

This is where compassion resides.

This is where unconditional love for self and others prevails.

Some may choose to use this knowledge, come out of their slumber, and question everything. However, some may fall into the trap of "Spirituality Sidestepping."

Glossary: Wtf Does That Mean: Spirituality Sidestepping

Spirituality Sidestepping is when you are still searching for something or someone outside of yourself to fix or save you, often replacing one rigid external belief system with another. There are several warning signs that you need to be aware of.

You still seek a teacher or guru to fix you.
    (Thinking: I can't do this on my own.)
You feel like you need an external doctrine to follow.
    (Thinking: Somebody just needs to tell me what to do, and I'll do it.)
You replace one set of rules with another set of rules.
    (Thinking: I need rules to follow to fix this mess I'm in.)
You criticize other religious or spiritual belief systems.
    (Thinking: Damn, those &&#@*, (fill in a religion), if they would just see the damage they are doing.)

If you resonate with any of these things, I encourage you to keep working to free yourself and align with your True Self. Even if you choose another program to study,

I intuitively know that one of the most effective ways to achieve world peace is by knowing your True Self. When your human self aligns with your True Self, aka spirit, you can see all the beauty that surrounds you, feel our interconnectedness, and not only talk about it, but actually LIVE it!

Hopefully you choose to embrace the journey of discovering your True Self with courage. By shedding the layers of bullsh*t programming and stepping into your authentic power, you not only heal yourself but also contribute to the healing of humanity. Your path to alignment is a powerful testament to the transformative potential that lies within us all. Let's explore how you can continue and deepen your journey with Souls Healing Humanity.

CHAPTER 17: THE JOURNEY CONTINUES

When you find yourself on the Alignment platform, and you will numerous times on your sojourn, you will understand how beautifully connected we are!

NOW! You respect all life and all choices.

NOW! You are no longer self-righteous and living with your finger pointing to all you perceive as "wrong."

NOW! You are aware. Accept and celebrate the incredible diversity that surrounds you.

NOW! You deeply understand that things are exactly as they need to be.

NOW! You have finally stopped struggling so much!

NOW! You understand that being in alignment with your True Self is key to World Peace.

While this book is coming to a close, your journey of self-discovery and transformation is far from over. This book is just the primer of the Holistic Scaffolding™ lifestyle. You have learned the basic tenets of each of the six platforms, but there is so much more to learn. (And, baby, I'm right there learning beside you!) It is essential to remember that although the platforms were presented in a linear fashion, you will utilize the Holistic Scaffolding™ in a natural and organic way, spending time on any platform at any time based on what you need.

You also have a fundamental understanding of how to create your life-altering plan by using:

Holistic Scaffolding™

"Do, Be and Become"

Assessments

Five Gold Golds
- *I choose to know the power of "I am."*
- *I choose to align with my True Self.*
- *I choose to Trust the Universe, Myself, and Others.*
- *I choose to be a "Lifelong Learner."*
- *I choose Love.*

Target Practice

Wisdom Nuggets

Wisdom Wands

If you're ready to fully craft your unique life-altering plan, consider participating in the online course: **Fed Up, Not F*cked Up**. Souls Healing Humanity also offers the **Fed Up, Not F*cked Up** companion workbook, which provides over 200 pages of journal prompts, activities, and Wisdom Wands.

By choosing this lifestyle, you will be well-equipped to handle anything life throws your way.
Your True Self, spirit, and soul have never been damaged, broken, or f*cked-up!

Wisdom Nugget:

You Are Who You've Been Looking For!

Hopefully, you find comfort in knowing that you need no one, but you are connected to everyone. So, keep "doing the work" to discover your True Self, and by doing so, you will create the most amazing life for yourself, and as a side benefit, you will be a soul that helps heal humanity.

I love all you people!

Love and ((HUGS)),
Laura

Printed in Great Britain
by Amazon